Garden Lattice Quilts

Eleanor Burns

for
Mother

First printing September, 2002

Published by Quilt in a Day®, Inc.
1955 Diamond St, San Marcos, CA 92069

©2002 by Eleanor A. Burns Family Trust

ISBN 1-891776-11-8

Art Director Merritt Voigtlander

Contents

Introduction

Garden Lattice is an adaptation of an old pattern called Betsy's Lattice, offered in newspapers by Laura Wheeler in the 1930's for just 10 cents. Readers were enticed to buy the pattern with this write-up: *Betsy's Lattice was hidden in an attic for many years, and only the enthusiasm of Laura Wheeler made its owner realize what a lovely old quilt she had. And with the enthusiasm went the wish – the ardent desire – to be able to offer this old-time pattern to quilt lovers. Besides being really most simple to do, it results in a quilt that has real decorative value, and although it is an old pattern, it is a bit different than those commonly seen.*

You won't need a green thumb to make this beautiful quilt! It's so much fun to bring your flower garden indoors, especially with the many beautiful florals available. Fat quarters and eighths are perfect. You begin by strip piecing 1½" strips for the Lattice (my favorite thing), and adding 6" squares cut into triangles for Sky or Flowers. Just sew the quarters together – the magic is in the locking seams! For those that enjoy applique, you can add fussy cut single flowers or clusters to the Lattice and stitch in vines to complete your garden.

The beauty of the block lies in its simplicity. By varying the fabrics, and placement of them, plus the addition of applique, different looks in overall quilt patterns are created.

When I taught Garden Lattice test classes to my students, they loved the creative ways they could embellish the simple blocks. They appliqued their favorite fabrics of flowers, fruits, birds, butterflies, and family pets into their gardens. I explained, "This is as arty as I get!" The creativity is all yours.

Gardening is now the number one hobby in America. Statistics show that 48% of quilters also love gardening. I know you will enjoy this quilt 100%!

Let your imagination grow!
Eleanor Burns

About the Quilts

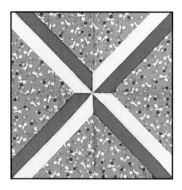

Identical Quarters

Blocks with Identical Quarters look old-fashioned sewn together into quilts. To create this design, you need four identical 6" squares and two 1½" Lattice strips for every block in your quilt. For larger quilts, make two blocks the same, and space them apart in the quilt.

Eleanor Burns – Twin   *Approximate Finished Size 63" x 87"*

Lattice
Select one color for the accent color in your quilt. In this example, red is the accent. Select a second color to contrast with the first, as muslin in this example, or one in a lighter value than the first. Both fabrics should be solid, or prints that appears solid from a distance.
In this example, a 1940's era was created with the red accent and reproduction feedsack prints.

Floral Triangles
Once you have decided on your color way, select different values of small and medium prints that include the Lattice accent color. Your quilt will coordinate easier if you begin with fabrics from the same line, and then add to them.

Border
Select any one of the fabrics used in the quilt.

Planned Quarters

Blocks with Planned Quarters look like an English Flower Garden with pathways between the flower beds. To create this design, you need two identical 6" floral squares and two different 1½" strips for Lattice per block. In addition, you need one matching 6" floral square to fill in the sides. All pieces must be laid out and planned before sewing any blocks together.

Lattice

Decide on one color for your accent. Select two different values of that color in fabrics that are solid, or prints that appear solid from a distance.

Floral Triangles

Once you have decided on your color way or theme, select floral fabrics in medium and large prints. Each print should have a touch of the accent color. Your quilt will coordinate easier if you begin with fabrics from the same line, and then add to them.

Border

Select one of the large scale prints used in the quilt.

Eleanor Burns – Lap　　　　*Approximate Finished Size 52" x 64"*

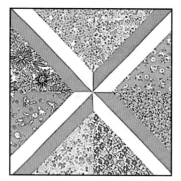

Scrappy Quarters for Quilt

Blocks with Scrappy Quarters use up all sorts of left-overs, and look very nostalgic. To create this design, you need two different 1½" Lattice strips per block, plus as many 6" squares as possible for variety in finished blocks. Set your theme through the fabric, as reproduction or contemporary.

Teresa Varnes – Queen

Approximate Finished Size 86" x 99"

Lattice
Select one fabric for the accent color in your quilt. In this example, a solid bubble gum pink was selected to set the nostalgic theme. Select a second solid, or a print that appears solid from a distance.

Floral Triangles
Once you decide on your theme or color way, select different values of those fabrics in small and medium prints, with each including a touch of the accent color. The quilt is more interesting with a variety of fabrics. The Lattice should pull all these fabrics together.

Border
Select any one of the fabrics used in quilt.

Scrappy Quarters for Garden

Blocks with Scrappy Quarters are best for artistic Gardens with flower appliques. Select two fabrics for 1½" Lattice strips and as many 6" squares as possible for variety in finished blocks.

Sky Triangles for Gardens

Decide on the time of day and scene you want to create, and then select those fabrics similar in color with slight variations in value. Contemporary prints that read solid from a distance work the best.

Applique

Select large scale flowers approximately 4" across with leaves attached that can be fussy cut as a single flower or a bunch of flowers. Fabrics printed in scale as birds, butterflies, cats, and dogs also add a charming touch.

Lattice

Decide on one color that will pull all your triangles together. Select two different values of that color in fabrics that are solid, or appear solid from a distance. In addition, a Base for the Garden is cut from the darkest Lattice.

Border

Select any one of the Sky fabrics used in the quilt.

Suzie SanNicolas – Nine Blocks   *Approximate Finished Size 47" x 49"*

Yardage Chart

	Four Block	Nine Block	Lap
Lattice			
#1 Lattice	½ yd (8) 1½" strips	¾ yd (13) 1½" strips	1 yd (17) 1 ½" strips
#2 Lattice	½ yd (8) 1½" strips	¾ yd (13) 1½" strips	1 yd (17) 1 ½" strips
Base for Garden Only (same as #2 Lattice)	⅛ yd (1) 3½" strip	¼ yd (1) 4½" strip	¼ yd (1) 4 ½" strip
Sky or Flowers			
	(16) fat ⅛ or ¼ yds (1) 6" sq from each or (16) 6" squares	(18) fat ⅛ or ¼ yds (2) 6" sqs from each or (36) 6" squares	(17) fat ⅛ or ¼ yds (3) 6" sqs from each or (48) 6" squares
Garden Quilts Only			
Large Scale Appliques *(Match Background of Flowers to Sky)*	1 yd	1½ yds	1½ yds
Light to Medium Weight Non-Woven Fusible Interfacing	1 yd	2 yds	2 yds
Paper Backed Fusible Web	1 yd	2 yds	2 yds
Cotton Batting for Stuffing	¼ yd	¼ yd	⅓ yd
Finishing			
Borders	⅝ yd (4) 4½" strips	¾ yd (5) 4½" strips	1¼ yd (6) 6½" strips
Binding	⅜ yd (4) 3" strips	½ yd (5) 3" strips	⅝ yd (6) 3" strips
Backing	1¼ yds	3 yds	4 yds
Batting	38" x 38"	54" x 54"	56" x 70"

		Blocks	Quilt	Garden
4 Block	4 Blocks 2 x 2	24" x 24"	34" x 34"	34" x 35"
9 Block	9 Blocks 3 x 3	36" x 36"	48" x 48"	48" x 50"
Lap	12 Blocks 3 x 4	36" x 48"	52" x 64"	52" x 66"
Twin	24 Blocks 4 x 6	48" x 72"	64" x 88"	64" x 90"
Queen	42 Blocks 6 x 7	72" x 84"	88" x 100"	88" x 102"
King	49 Blocks 7 x 7	84" x 84"	100" x 100"	100" x 102"

Twin	Queen	King
1½ yds (31) 1½" strips	2¼ yds (51) 1½" strips	2¾ yds (58) 1½" strips
1½ yds (31) 1½" strips	2¼ yds (51) 1½" strips	2¾ yds (58) 1½" strips
⅓ yd (2) 4½" strips	⅓ yd (2) 4½" strips	⅓ yd (2) 4½" strips
(24) ¼ yds (4) 6" sqs from each or (96) 6" squares	(21) ⅜ yds (8) 6" sqs from each or (168) 6" squares	(25) ⅜ yds (8) 6" sqs from each or (196) 6" squares
2 yds	2 yds	2½ yds
3 yds	3 yds	3 yds
3 yds	3 yds	3 yds
½ yd	½ yd	½ yd
1½ yds (8) 6½" strips	2 yds (10) 6½" strips	2⅛ yds (11) 6½" strips
¾ yd (8) 3" strips	1 yd (10) 3" strips	1 yd (11) 3" strips
5½ yds	8 yds	9 yds
70" x 96"	96" x 110"	110" x 110"

Supplies

Rotary Cutter

6" x 24" ruler or Shape Cut™

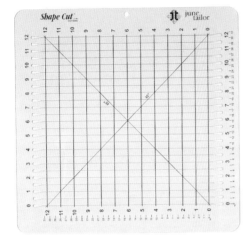

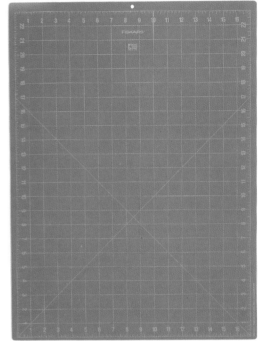

10" x 12" Cutting Mat and 18" x 24 Cutting Mat

6½" Triangle Square Up Ruler

Place sandpaper dots on under side so ruler doesn't slip.

Applique Supplies

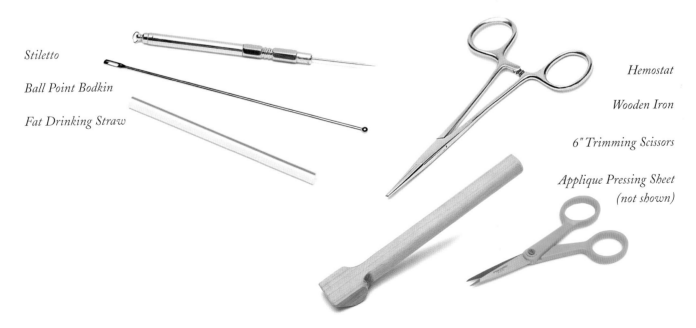

Stiletto

Ball Point Bodkin

Fat Drinking Straw

Hemostat

Wooden Iron

6" Trimming Scissors

Applique Pressing Sheet (not shown)

Cutting

Cut Lattice into 1½" wide selvage to selvage strips.
Cut Floral or Sky fabrics into 6" squares. Use a ruler,
rotary cutter, and cutting mat, or a rotary cutter and
Shape Cut™ by June Tailor. Photographs show how
to use a Shape Cut™.

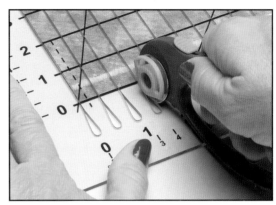

Line up zero horizontal line with bottom edge of fabric.

Cutting 1½" Strips

1. Fold Lattice fabric into fourths, lining up selvage edges with fold.

2. Place Shape Cut™ on fabric. Line up zero horizontal line with bottom edge of fabric. Allow
   extra fabric to left of zero for straightening.

3. Place blade of cutter in zero line, and straight-
   en left edge of fabric. Cut strips every 1½".

4. Cut Borders according to Yardage Charts.

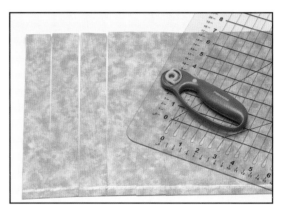

Cut Lattice fabric into 1½" strips.

Cutting 6" Squares

1. Fold Floral or Sky fabric into fourths.

2. Square off left edge, and cut into 6" strips.

3. Turn strip, square off left edge, and cut
   into 6" squares.

Cut Flowers or Sky fabric into 6" strips.

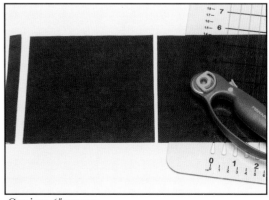

Cut into 6" squares.

Sewing Blocks

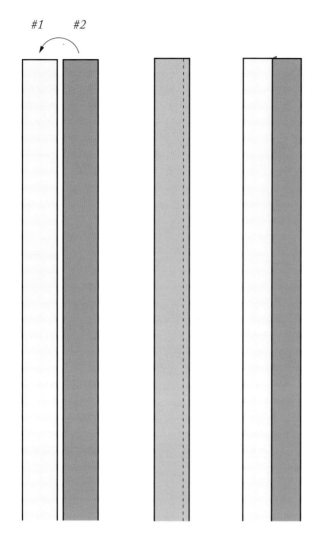

1. Set aside #1 and #2 Lattice for your Framing Border.

4 Block	4 each
9 Block	4 each
Lap	5 each
Twin	7 each
Queen	9 each
King	9 each

2. Stack remaining #1 and #2 Lattice strips right side up. Place darkest Lattice strip on right.

3. Flip top strip on right to top strip on left, right sides together. Line up outside edges.

4. Assembly-line sew with accurate and consistent ¼" seam and 15 stitches to the inch, or 2.0 setting on computerized sewing machine.

5. Place strip set on pressing mat with darkest fabric on top. Line up strip with lines on pressing mat.

6. Set seam.

7. Open and press against seam. Seam should be behind darkest strip.

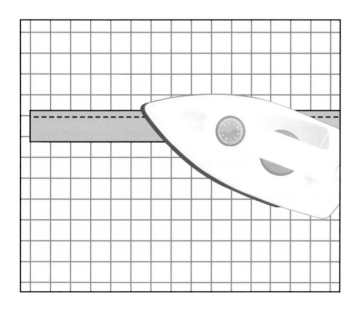

8. Fold strip in half lengthwise.

9. Fold in half again.

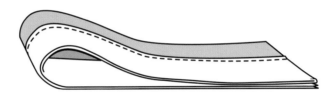

10. Fold in half again so piece is approximately 5" - 5½" in length. Steam press edges.

11. Open strip and check that there are seven crease marks.

Pressing and Cutting 6" Squares

1. Stack two Sky or Flower squares right sides up.

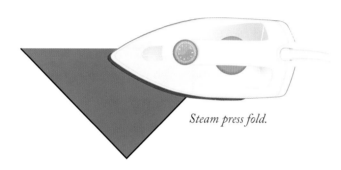

Steam press fold.

2. Fold in half on diagonal, right sides together.

3. Steam press fold to create a match point for Lattice strips

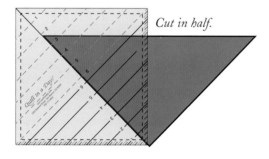

Cut in half.

4. Place 6½" ruler's 45° line on folded squares and cut in half.

Stack in two piles.

5. Stack in two separate piles right side up.

6. Keep identical triangles together.

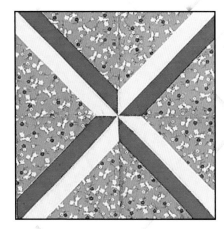

Identical Quarters

Turn to
page 20.

Scrappy Quarters

Turn to
page 20.

Planned Quarters

Continue on
pages 18 and 19.

Laying Out Planned Blocks

Use a large floor area or design wall.

1. Open pressed strip. Cut every other fold so strips are approximately 10" long.

Example is for a Four Block.

2. Lay out four Lattice strips in X pattern for first block. Carefully place #2 darkest Lattice.

3. Lay out remaining Lattice strips in block formation for your size quilt.

Four Block	2 x 2
Nine Block	3 x 3
Lap	3 x 4
Twin	4 x 6
Queen	6 x 7
King	7 x 7

4. Place four triangles of same Flower fabric inside Lattice.

5. Place two triangles of same Flower fabric on outside edge.

6. Continue until all spaces are filled.

This is an example of a Four Block quilt.

7. Slide one block onto large cutting mat and place it next to sewing machine.

8. Starting in the upper left corner, flip #1 Triangle right sides together to darkest Lattice strip, and center.

9. Continuing in counter-clock wise order, flip #2 Triangle right sides together to darkest Lattice strip. Continue with #3 and #4 Triangles.

10. Stack Triangles with strips. Follow sewing directions on pages 20-28.

11. Place back in block layout for placement of remaining Triangles #5,6,7, and 8 on lightest Lattice strip.

12. Sew complete block together before laying out next block.

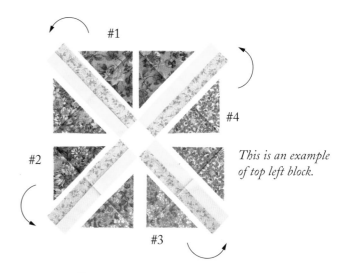

This is an example of top left block.

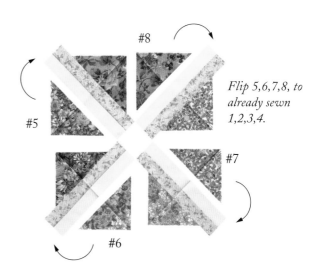

Flip 5,6,7,8, to already sewn 1,2,3,4.

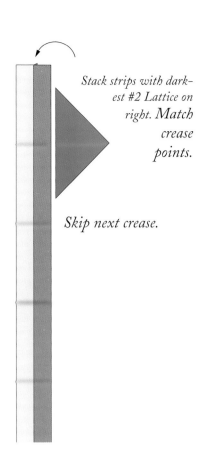

Stack strips with darkest #2 Lattice on right. Match crease points.

Skip next crease.

Sewing First Triangles to Lattice

1. Stack strips with darkest #2 Lattice on right.

2. Stack triangles to right of Lattice.

3. Flip triangle right sides together to strip, matching first crease point on strip with crease point on triangle. Sew triangle to strip.

4. Skip next crease.

5. Flip triangle to third crease on strip, and sew.

6. Continue to assembly-line sew triangles to darkest side of strips. Four triangles fit on each strip.

Identical: Sew same four triangles in a row.

Scrappy: Mix up triangles and sew.

Planned: Sew four triangles as placed on strips.

Pressing First Triangles

1. Place strip set on pressing mat with triangles on top. Set seam.

2. Open, and press against triangle. Avoid pressing crease marks on strip and triangles.

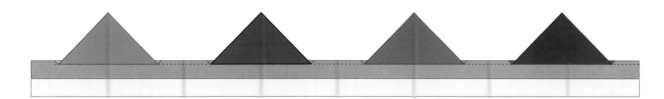

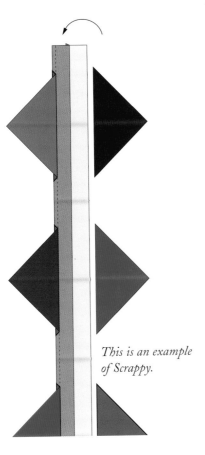

This is an example of Scrappy.

Sewing Second Set of Triangles

1. Place strip with light #1 Lattice under presser foot and stack of triangles on right.

2. Flip triangle right sides together to strip, matching crease points.

3. Assembly-line sew triangles to strips.

Identical: Use same triangle as one directly across on strip.

Scrappy: Use a different triangle than the one directly across on the strip.

Planned: Sew together according to block layout.

Pressing Second Triangles

Seams are pressed in same direction, so when blocks are sewn together, every seam locks.

1. Cut strips apart on fold lines between blocks.

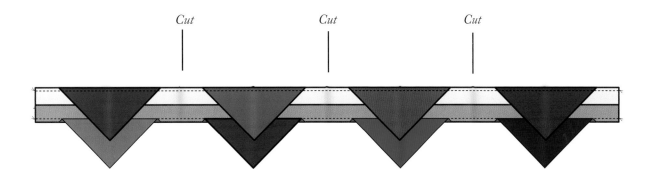

Cut *Cut* *Cut*

2. Stack.

3. Turn stack over so lightest #1 Lattice strip is across top.

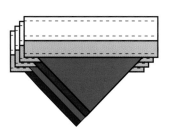

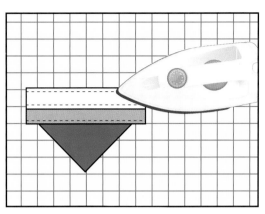

Set seams with lightest strip on top.

4. Set seam.

5. Open, and press against lightest #1 Lattice strip.

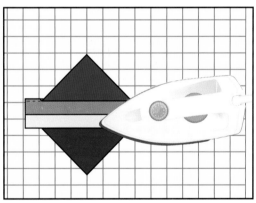

6. Turn pieces over and check from wrong side.

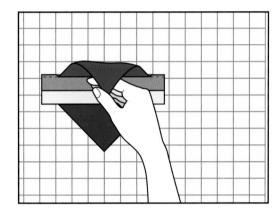

Open and press toward strip.

7. Center seams are pressed toward darkest strip. **All seams should be going in same direction.**

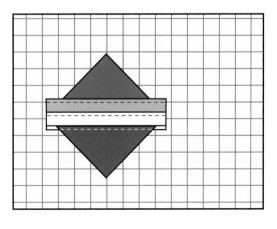

Squaring Quarter Patch to 6½"

1. Place quarter patch on 10" x 12" cutting mat right side up.

2. Center 6½" Triangle Square Up ruler on patch. Match center diagonal line on ruler with center seam.

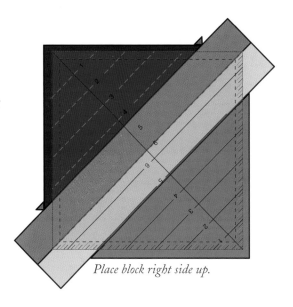

Place block right side up.

3. If you are right handed, trim right and top sides of block. If you are left handed, trim left and top sides of block.

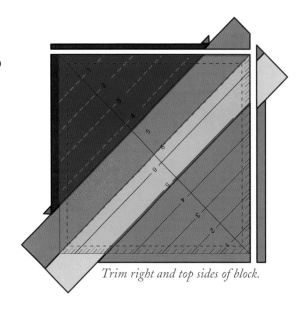

Trim right and top sides of block.

4. Rotate mat, and trim remaining two sides so patch is 6½" square.

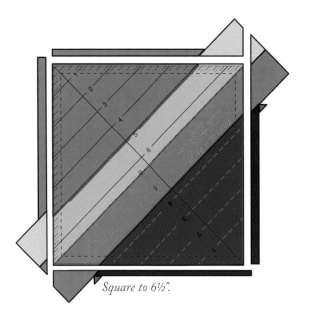

Square to 6½".

Sewing Four Quarters Together

1. Lay out your quarters and plan placement.

2. Make four stacks of patches equal to the total number of blocks.
   Carefully turn #2 Lattice as illustrated.

3. Flip top patch on right to top patch on left. Check that seams go in opposite directions.

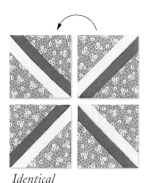

Identical

Scrappy

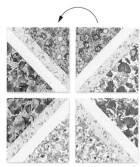

Planned

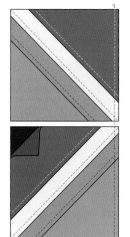

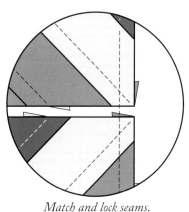

Match and lock seams.

4. Match and lock seams.

5. Assembly-line sew blocks together.

6. Clip apart between blocks.

7. Stack pairs of joined quarters.

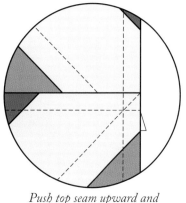

Push top seam upward and underneath seam downward.

8. Open and flip pairs of quarters right side together. **Push top seam upward and underneath seam downward.**

9. Lock and sew matching center seams. Hold seams flat with stiletto.

10. Assembly-line sew blocks.

11. Check that new seam crosses at "V" on both sides.

Unsewing

1. At the center seam, cut the first stitch with scissors.

2. Remove the two or three **vertical stitches** at the center with stiletto or seam ripper.

3. Turn block over, and repeat removing vertical stitches at center.

4. Open the center seams and push down flat to form a tiny pinwheel.

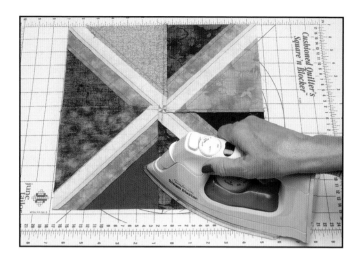

5. From the wrong side, press new seams clockwise around the block.

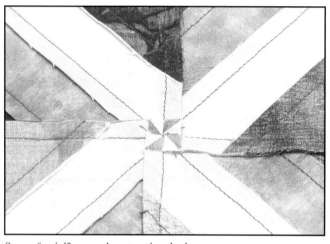

6. Make sure that seams "swirl" around center pinwheel.

7. Press from the right side.

Seams "swirl" around center pinwheel.

8. Lay out blocks in order.

Four Block	2 x 2
Nine Block	3 x 3
Lap	3 x 4
Twin	4 x 6
Queen	6 x 7
King	7 x 7

9. Assembly-line sew vertical rows, sewing seams as pressed. Do not clip connecting threads.

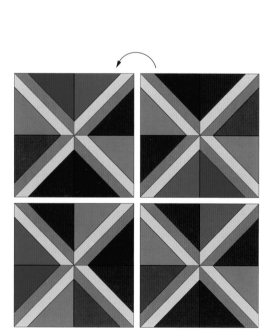

10. Sew horizontal rows, pushing seams in opposite directions at connecting threads.

Framing Border

Gardens have a Framing Border on three sides. The Base is sewn to the fourth side.

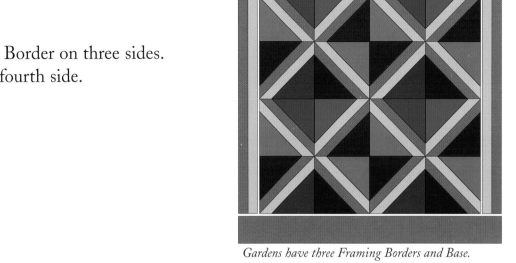

Gardens have three Framing Borders and Base.

Quilts have a Framing Border on all four sides.

Quilts have a Framing Border on all four sides.

Piecing Framing Border

1. For all quilts larger than nine blocks, piece remaining #1 Lattice and #2 Lattice into **long strips.**

2. Sew #1 and #2 Lattice strips together.

3. Set seams with #2 Lattice strip on top. Open and press seams toward #2.

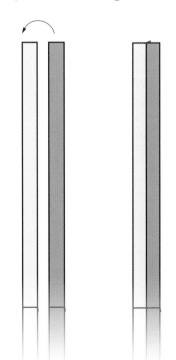

Sew Lattice into long strips.

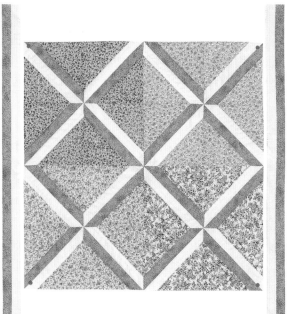

Mitering Framing Border

Garden

1. **Mark dots ¼" from corners** on top left and top right of Garden.

2. Place Lattice strips on sides, placing lightest #1 Lattice next to sides.

3. Allow 4" at top. Trim to match bottom edge.

Quilt

1. **Mark dots ¼" from all four corners.**

2. Place Lattice strips on sides, placing lightest #1 Lattice next to quilt.

3. Allow 4" at top and 4" at bottom for miter.

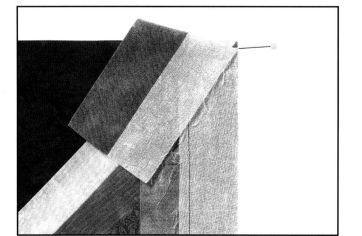

Sewing Mitered Corners

1. Flip Lattice right sides together and pin, beginning at ¼" mark.

2. Sew Lattice to sides, leaving ¼" open.

3. Set seams with Lattice on top. Open, and press toward Lattice.

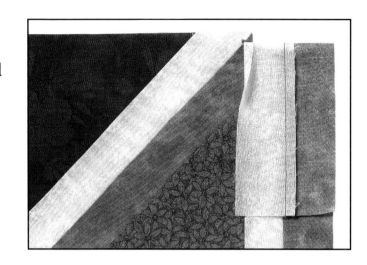

4. Flip Side Lattice out of way. Fold Top Lattice in half. Match Lattice to center.

Match Center

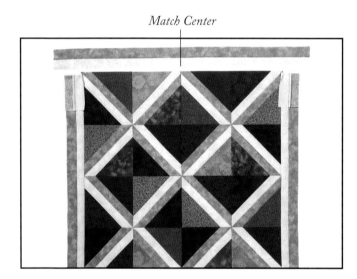

5. Pin Top Lattice to quilt. Allow 4" to extend on both sides. Sew, leaving ¼" open on both ends.

6. **Quilt: Repeat on bottom.**

7. Set seam with Lattice on top, open, and press toward Lattice.

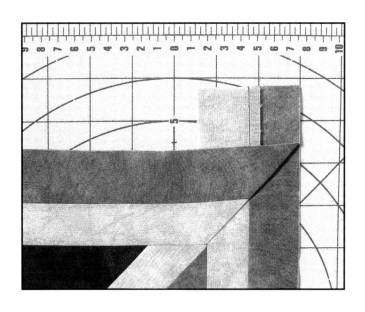

8. Place corner on pressing mat. Lay bottom strip out flat. Fold top strip under at 45° angle. Match ends of strips.

9. Press.

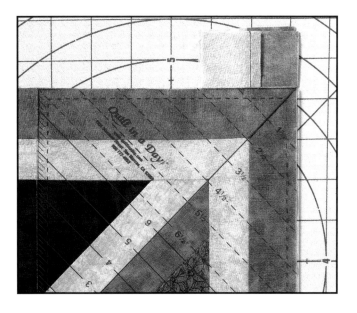

10. Check angle with 6½" Triangle Square Up ruler.

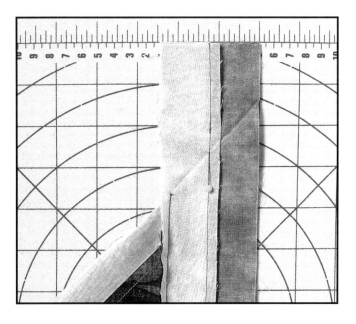

11. Carefully open pressed corner. Pin on creased line, matching seams.

12. Sew on creased line beginning at open ¼". Open and check that seams line up.

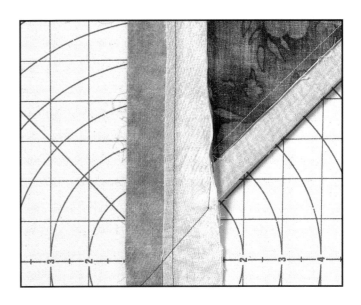

13. Trim ¼" from seam.

14. Press seam open. Trim tips from corner.

Adding Base Strip to Garden

1. Sew base strip from Lattice #2 fabric to bottom. Strip will be 3½" or 4½" wide depending on size of top.

2. Set seam with base strip on top.

3. Open and press toward strip.

Adding Borders

1. Measure sides. Cut two Borders that length.

2. Pin and sew to sides. Set seam with Border on top. Open, and press toward Border.

3. Measure top. Cut Border that length. Pin and sew.

4. Set seam with Border on top. Open, and press toward Border.

5. **Quilt: Add fourth Border.**

Applique for Garden Quilt

There are several different materials used to make your flowers and other shapes. Methods can be mixed in the same quilt.

- Paper Backed Fusible Web — page 35
- Non-Woven Fusible Interfacing — page 36
- Fabric Backing — page 36

Paper Back Fusible Web

This is the fastest method. Raw outside edges are finished with free-motion stitching. Steam-A-Seam 2® has a pressure sensitive coating on both sides which allows for a temporary hold until pressed with an iron.

1. Press fusible side of product to wrong side of fabric. Follow directions on package.

Press fusible side of product to wrong side of fabric. Use electronic press or iron.

2. Cut around shape on outside edge.

Cut around shape on outside edge.

3. Peel remaining paper away.

4. Position and pin to top.

5. When all flowers are arranged, press to quilt top with iron or electronic press following manufacturer's directions.

Peel paper away.

Fusible Interfacing or Fabric

Shapes with straight edges can be used along bottom.

This is the more time consuming method, but outside edges are finished, and can be "stuffed" for additional dimension.

1. Rough cut fabric shapes ½" from design, and place on quilt top. Plan where finished shapes will be finally placed. Shapes with straight edges can be used along bottom.

2. Place right side of fabric against rough, fusible side of fusible interfacing, or right side of backing fabric. Pin. Cut interfacing or backing same size as fabric shape.

3. If shape outline is too faint to see, trace outline of shape with permanent marking pen.

4. Place open toe foot on sewing machine. Change to 18 stitches per inch, or 1.8 on computerized sewing machine. If possible, reduce pressure on presser foot.

5. Sew around shapes with fabric on top. If background matches Sky, it's not necessary to sew meticulously around details.

6. Trim seams to ⅛". Clip inside curves.

7. Cut small opening in center of interfacing, or backing. Cut drinking straw in half. Insert straw into hole.

8. Push straw against fabric. Place ball of bodkin on fabric stretched over straw. Gently push fabric into straw with bodkin to start turning piece.

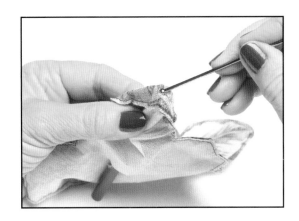

9. Remove straw and bodkin. Shape should be partially turned.

10. Continue turning with straw and bodkin until shape is completely turned right side out.

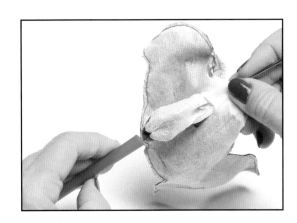

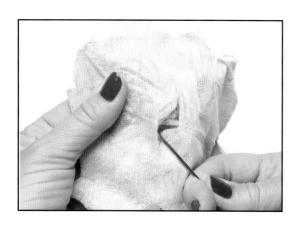

11. Run bodkin around inside edge, pushing out seams.

12. Gently pick out sharp points with stiletto.

13. From right side, push fabric over edge with wooden iron.

14. Pin shape on firm 100% cotton batting, and cut batting same size as shape.

15. Insert batting though opening with hemostat.

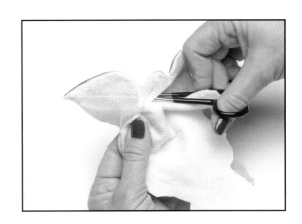

16. Place darning foot on sewing machine. Drop feed dogs. Select coordinating thread.

17. Free motion outline stitch on design of shape. *Heavy quilting once shapes are fused in place draws up bottom of quilt.*

If necessary, pin small shapes to stabilizer so you have something to hold onto while free motion stitching.

18. Place quilt on design wall. Place shapes with straight, open edges across bottom. Line up raw edges. Position additional shapes across bottom and trailing along Lattice.

19. Prepare large pieces of shapes to flow over Borders.

20. Steam press shapes in place. Use steam iron or electronic press.

21. Press from wrong side.

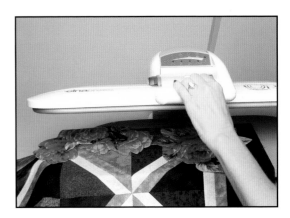

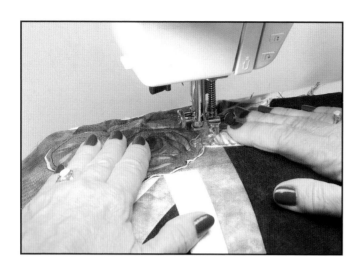

22. Sew around outside edges of shapes by hand or free motion machine stitch.

Machine stitching can also be completed after top is layered with Batting and Backing.

23. Measure, pin and sew Border to bottom of quilt.

24. Set seams, open, and press toward Border.

25. Place additional shapes across bottom Border seam.

"Wannabe" gardeners Teresa, Patricia, and Eleanor team sewed flowers on fusible interfacing, and stuffed them.

Keeping the garden plot in the family, cousin Carol Selepec added dimension to the stuffed flowers with free motion stitching around the designs with her long arm quilting machine.

Just sniff the fragrance coming from the flowers!

Finishing Your Quilt

Layering the Quilt

1. Spread out Backing on a large table or floor area, right side down. Clamp fabric to edge of table with quilt clips, or tape Backing to the floor. Do not stretch Backing.

2. Layer the Batting on the Backing and pat flat.

3. With quilt right side up, center on the Backing. Smooth until all layers are flat. Clamp or tape outside edges.

Safety Pinning

1. Place pin covers on 1" safety pins. Safety pin through all layers three to five inches apart. Pin away from where you plan to quilt.

2. Catch tip of pin in grooves on pinning tool, and close pins.

3. Use pinning tool to open pins when removing them. Store pins opened.

"Stitch in the Ditch" along Lattice, Triangles and Borders

1. Thread your machine with matching thread or invisible thread. If you use invisible thread, loosen your top tension. Match the bobbin thread to the Backing.

2. Attach your walking foot, and lengthen the stitch to 8 to 10 stitches per inch or 3.5 on computerized machines.

3. Tightly roll quilt on diagonal to #1. Place hands on quilt in triangular shape, and spread seams open. Stitch in the ditch continuously on seam lines, starting at #1 and following the arrows to #12. Use needle down feature on sewing machine if available, and pivot with needle in fabric.

4. Move quilt to #13 and stitch continuously until all seam lines are quilted.

5. Optional: Stitch around blocks on point.

Stitch around blocks on point.

Binding

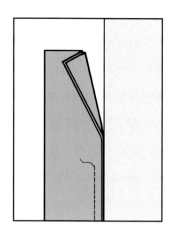

1. Place a walking foot attachment on your sewing machine and regular thread on top and in the bobbin to match the Binding.

2. Square off the selvage edges, and sew 3" Binding strips together lengthwise. Fold and press in half with wrong sides together.

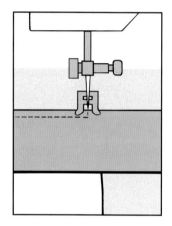

3. Line up the raw edges of the folded Binding with the raw edges of the quilt in the middle of one side. Begin stitching 4" from the end of the Binding. Sew with 10 stitches per inch, or 3.0 to 3.5. Sew ⅜" from edge, or width of walking foot.

4. At the corner, stop the stitching ⅜" in from the edge with the needle in the fabric. Raise the presser foot and turn the quilt to the next side. Put the foot back down. Stitch backwards off the edge of the Binding.

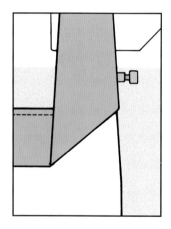

5. Raise the foot, and pull the quilt forward slightly. Fold the Binding strip straight up on the diagonal. Fingerpress the diagonal fold.

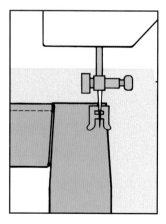

6. Fold the Binding strip straight down with the diagonal fold underneath. Line up the top of the fold with the raw edge of the Binding underneath.

7. Begin sewing from the edge.

8. Continue stitching and mitering the corners around the outside of the quilt.

9. Stop stitching 4" from where the ends will overlap.

10. Line up the two ends of Binding. Trim the excess with a ½" overlap.

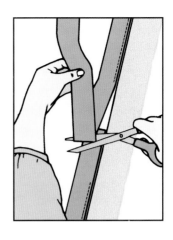

11. Open out the folded ends and pin right sides together. Sew a ¼" seam.

12. Continue stitching Binding in place.

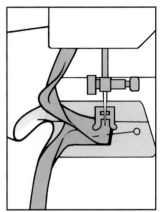

13. Trim the Batting and Backing up to ⅛" from the raw edges of the Binding.

14. Fold the Binding to the back side of the quilt. Pin in place so that the folded edge on the Binding covers the stitching line. Tuck in the excess fabric at each miter on the diagonal.

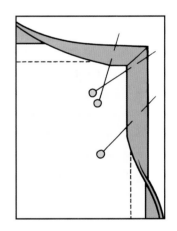

15. From the right side, "stitch in the ditch" using invisible thread on the front side, and bobbin thread to match the Binding on the back side. Catch the folded edge of the Binding on the back side with the stitching.

    Optional: Hand stitch Binding in place.

16. Sew an identification label on the Back.

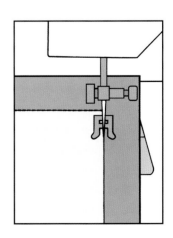

Index

Jane Burger's Bug Quilt is a favorite with her young sons, Cody and Reilly. Jane kept her boys entertained on fabric shopping sprees with the promise that if they behaved, they could select their favorite bug fabrics. Looks like Jane has two great sons! Older daughter Ashley also loves to make quilts.

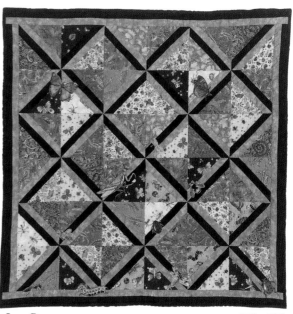

Jane Burger   *37" x 37"*

Acknowledgements

Bouquets of Flowers to Quiltmakers

Yvonne Barcelona
Sue Bouchard
Jane Burger
Robin Grube
Patricia Knoechel
Roberta Mileski
Suzie SanNicolas
Carol Selepec
Sandy Thompson
Melissa Varnes
Teresa Varnes

Cover photograph location

Hill Street Coffee House, Oceanside, CA.

Fifteen year old Melissa Varnes was ecstatic as her planned Garden Lattice Quilt came together. Her vision was to permanently capture the gorgeous California coast line in fabric. She generously gave her landscape treasure, the second quilt she's made, to good friend Sean Fresh. He's proud of her perfect matches!

Melissa Varnes - Twin   *62" x 86"*

Order Information

Quilt in a Day books offer a wide range of techniques and are directed toward a variety of skill levels. If you do not have a quilt shop in your area, you may write or call for a complete catalog and current price list of all books and patterns published by Quilt in a Day®, Inc.

Quilt in a Day®, Inc. • 1955 Diamond Street • San Marcos, CA 92069
1 800 777-4852 • Fax: (760) 591-4424 • www.quiltinaday.com

Yvonne Barcelona created the look of a patio garden in her quilt. Vibrant wisteria dangle from a vine growing across the top of the garden lattice. Calla lilies grow from a clay pot while curious Kitty eyes a hummingbird nearby! Red tea roses wind their way up from the bottom of the lattice. Resting by the pot is Kikki, Yvonne's pet sheltie . Yvonne used paper backed fusing to hold her intricate fabric flowers in place, and then free motion stitched around the outside edges. Notice how she shaded her sky triangles from light at the top, down to dark at the bottom.